Joy Beyond Grief

Joy Beyond Grief

By COLENA M. ANDERSON

**ZONDERVAN PUBLISHING HOUSE** OF THE ZONDERVAN CORPORATION GRAND RAPIDS, MICHIGAN 49506

Scripture quotations are from the *Revised Standard Version,* copyright
1946 (renewed © 1973), 1952 and © 1971 by Division of Christian Education of
the National Council of Churches of Christ in the United States of America.
Used by permission of the Division of Christian Education, National Council
of Churches. Zondervan Publishing House, Licensee.

Second printing   1979
This edition   1979

Library of Congress Cataloging in Publication Data

Anderson, Colena M
   Joy beyond grief.

   1.   Consolation.   I.   Title.
BV4905.2.A52 1979   248'.86   78-31189
ISBN 0-310-20041-5

ISBN 0-310-20041-5/0395

Printed in the United States of America

To

Elam
and
our children:
Frances
Victor
Elam

Contents

Yes, I Know / 11

Stations of Grief / 15

Emotional Numbers / 23

The Sympathizing Thought / 33

The Special Days / 43

The Thin Veil / 51

The Quickening / 63

Renewal / 69

Yes, I Know

Yes, I Know

As soon as the news of George's death was relayed to me, I hurried to see Nellie, his wife — no, now she was his widow.

Our minister and two neighbors were there.

"Thank God, you've come," one neighbor said.

"You're the one she needs now," said the other.

Both went to Nellie, touched her, said, "We'll be back later," and left the room.

I dropped on my knees beside Nellie and put my arms around her.

"I'll leave, too," said the minister. "You know better than I what to say to her now."

Say to her? There was little I could say. The most I could do was feel.

Nellie buried her head on my shoulder and through her tears whispered, "You know. You know."

"Yes, I know." How well I knew!

This stark knowledge had come to me on a summer morning in 1944, a year before this day with Nellie. It was as fresh now as then.

Nellie, at least, had had some warning, for George had been in the hospital in intensive care for several days. I had had no warning, no preparation. But with or without warning, death is always a painful shock.

In a split second there at Nellie's side, the last twenty-four hours of my own husband's life passed in swift review, as they had countless times since that mid-August morning.

On Wednesday morning at family devotions Elam was reading:

Then I saw a new heaven and a new earth; for the first heaven and the first earth had passed away, and the sea was no more. And I saw the holy city, new Jerusalem, coming down out of heaven from God, prepared as a bride adorned for her husband; and I heard a great voice from the throne saying, "Behold, the dwelling of God is with men. He will dwell with them, and they shall be his people, and God himself will be with *them; he will wipe away every tear from their eyes, and death shall be no more, neither shall there be mourning nor crying nor pain any more, for the former things have passed away."*

And he who sat upon the throne said, "Behold, I make all things new." Also he said, "Write this, for these words are trustworthy and true."

(Revelation 21: 1-5)

Then while he brought the car from the garage to go to the office, I went out to the garden to gather greens and flowers for the house. I hoped the greens would last for the faculty dinner on Friday, two days away. When he came up from the garage, I had a bunch of sweet geraniums in my arms. As we kissed good-by, close to each other, the leaves crushed, releasing their fragrance.

That evening at a garden dinner I met his gaze and, reading the well-known message, I felt my pulse quicken. Later, apart from the others, we stood a short while by ourselves. Contemplating a neighbor's house overrun by red ramblers in full bloom, he said, his arm tightening about me, "When I retire, we'll have a place like that."

Back home after dinner, he asked to hear the ending of a story, "The Fifth Blessing," that I had been writing about an old Chinese servant during the bombing of Chungking. The title was taken from the Chinese "Five Blessings": Long Life, Wealth, Happiness, Rank, and a Peaceful Passing from the Earth.

"But you're too tired," I said.

"No, I want to hear it," he insisted.

So I read the revised ending where Lao Wang, the old servant, holding in his arms the newly born son of the missionaries for whom he had worked, said, "Now lettest thou thy servant depart in peace." Then he gave the baby back to the mother and moved away. Within minutes a rock, loosened by the bombing, fell and killed him.

"This is a better ending than your first," said Elam. "Truly a fifth blessing for Lao Wang. He never knew what struck him."

"He never knew what struck him." Not Wednesday evening now, but early Thursday morning, and not Elam's voice, but the doctor's. He had his hand on my shoulder. He was saying, "He never knew." Then, "You're strong. You'll make it."

"You're strong!" he said to me who had wakened less than half an hour ago to find Elam in the adjacent room — lifeless. Strong! I — a widow.

I tightened my hold on Nellie and patted her shoulder. Again I said, "I know. Yes, I know." Then, more softly, "God bless you and lead you through the valley."

As now, at the beginning of this book, I say to every widow or widower who reads it, "God bless you and lead you through your valley."

Stations of Grief

Stations of Grief

The Lamentations of Jeremiah open with the lines:

> **How lonely sits the city**
> **that was full of people!**
> **How like a widow has she become,**
> **she that was great among the**
> **nations!**
>
> (Lamentations 1:1)

In his exposition of this Old Testament book, one commentator exclaims, "One wonders how many ever read this book!" and asks, "Why should such a book be in the Bible? Just a series of heartbroken cries, one might say."

His answer is, "It is indeed so easy to be careless and blithe in the presence of human misery that we need reminders of the solemn fact that there is much in human life that calls for sorrow."[1]

That answer is valid for many persons, but not for us widows. We need no reminders. In our fresh grief, we are no longer in the presence of human misery.

All of human misery is within us, "pressed down, shaken together, running over," a good measure, but not a measure of good. Body, mind, and soul are turgid with it. The series of cries in Lamentations are not for Jerusalem, sacked by the Babylonians thousands of years ago; they are for ourselves today.

Persons who in the past few decades have seen cities or pictures of cities destroyed by war can readily imagine the houses of long-ago Jerusalem turned to rubble, its streets obliterated, the temple in ruins, signs of fire and carnage, the sinews of the city twisted, broken, and laid waste. To such a city the writer of Lamentations makes his comparison, "How like a widow!"

Contemplating the simile, a widow reverses it and cries, "How like a devastated city now am I!" She identifies with the destroyed city. She sees her own condition reflected in the verses.

Tears, restlessness, desolation, loss of status, the pain of memories, scorn, self-pity, and self-blame — these are her personal experiences. They are the stations of grief on her sad, solitary journey.

~ ℰ·ℰ ~

Tears

She weeps bitterly in the night, tears on her cheeks.

(Lamentations 1:2)

Who among us has not wept bitterly in the night? Who can hold back tears when joy has dimmed?

~ ℰ·ℰ ~

Withdrawal

Judah has gone into exile because of affliction.

(Lamentations 1:3)

Tempted for a time to isolate ourselves from people and from the world, we long for retreat, a place to go apart, a small spot away from everybody. "Oh, leave me alone!" is the cry of our hearts.

~ ℰ·ℰ ~

Restlessness

She dwells now among the nations, but finds no resting place.

(Lamentations 1:3)

Yearn as much as we may to withdraw from others, we must still dwell among our friends and neighbors and in the midst of our families. The only possible exile is a sanitarium, and there we must dwell among doctors and nurses. For a time there is no resting place, none by day and none by night. We walk through the rooms as tigers and bears walk in a zoo — restless, restless. We lie down to sleep and our dreams are filled with searching, but never finding.

~ ℰ·ℰ ~

Desolation

All her gates are desolate.

(Lamentations 1:4)

How desolate indeed the gates, the doors through which he will never again enter! Will you ever forget that last time he left the house? And the first time you entered the house after his final leaving?

I have not forgotten. Still as fresh as though it had happened this morning is the memory of that sudden weakness that overtook me at my first entry. Had it not been for the quick support of my sons on either side of me, I should have fallen on the steps. Even with all my family around me, so desolate was that familiar entryway that I could not pass through unaided.

Pearl Buck writes of this experience: "But oh, that silent last moment, when he must be left behind, and the arrival at the house, now empty! Of these I cannot speak. To other women in like circumstances, who may read these pages, I can only say there is no escape from such moments when they come. They must be lived through, not once, but many times in memory."[2]

❦

Loss of Status

From the daughter of Zion has departed all her majesty.
(Lamentations 1:6)

Widows are not queens. But in spite of present advances in women's liberation, we are still for the most part women who derived status from our married state. Note how, even though *Ms* pushes itself into circulation, social etiquette decrees that a widow retain her husband's name. We are told, "On the Social Register there is no such person as Mrs. Joan Doe. Wife or widow, a woman is Mrs. Joseph Doe."

And note the state of affairs at a store where the charge cards are always issued in the husband's name. How painfully difficult it is for any woman who is divorced, separated, or widowed to get credit in her own name, even though she may have a full-time, well-paying job, a savings account, and substantial possessions![3]

Over and over again widows complain, "After my husband died, I became a Nobody. When he was alive, I was a Somebody. I was 'the wife of _____.'"

"When he was the speaker at a banquet," said Sarah, "I was placed at the head table too. Now — ." But she didn't need to continue. Everybody at the banquet last week knew where she sat. At a table near the door. The wife of the man taking her husband's place was at the head table.

Eleanor Roosevelt assumed that there would be a loss of status after President Roosevelt's death. After the funeral, when Henry Morgenthau, Jr. urged her to settle her affairs as quickly as possible so that she might speak to the world in her own right, she "sort of questioned whether now that she was the widow of the President anybody would want to hear her."[4]

❦

Memories

**Jerusalem remembers in the days
of her affliction and bitterness
All the precious things
that were hers in the days of old.**
(Lamentations 1:7)

Part of the joy of life together used to be remembering what we did on anniversaries matching the current one, where we spent past holidays, how we planned together the surprise gifts for the children, the sparkle of little jokes we played on each other: he to me, "Remember when you. . . ." I to him, "Remember when you . . . ." Happy days of remembering then when we remembered together!

But now we must remember alone and find that memories compound our grief. Now we know as we've never known before "that a widow's crown of sorrow is remembering happier things." When we bemoan these memories to family and friends, we soon hear their admonitions, given kindly or sternly, "What's past is past. Don't brood about what's gone. What good is there in torturing yourself with what never again can be?"

Those words, "Never again"! They cut like a knife. No longer for us are the "saddest words of tongue or pen 'It might have been,'" but "Never again."

There are, of course, many changes in life other than the great change that comes with death. Life is in a constant state of flux which we accept with reasonable equanimity until we come to one moment when we cry out, "If only I could hold this forever."

Long years ago my mother came to such a moment which she remembered all through her life, and with which she used to try to comfort me when in my youth I became distressed over moving from one house to another or having a friend move out of town.

"One early evening," she would recall, "when you were a baby, daddy and you and I were sitting around the kitchen table. We had finished supper. I was sewing a dress for you. He was peeling apples. You were in your high chair holding out your little hand for 'Mo, Mo' of the tiny pieces of apple. The lighted kerosene lamp was on the table. I can still see how real the roses on the shade looked. Close by, the kitchen stove was warming the room. Outside, the autumn rain was running down the gutter, and now and then a branch of the willow tree was blown against the house. A small storm outside, but oh, so cozy inside!

"'Oh, Charlie,' I said, my throat tightening, 'I wish I could keep this moment forever and ever.'

"Then daddy said, 'But you know, Frankie, you can't. And you really wouldn't want us to stay this way forever. You want the baby to grow up, don't you?'"

Of course she did. Yet in those thirty-one years since my father's death when mother lived with me, including the twenty-two years since Elam's death, neither she nor I failed to feel a tightening of the throat whenever she sang to my accompaniment the German song:

Es kann nicht immer so bleiben
hier unter dem wechzelnden Mond;
es bluht eine Zeit und verwelket,
was mit uns die Erde bewohnt,
was mit uns die Erde bewohnt.[5]

Things can never stay the same
here under the changing moon;
all that inhabits this earth
flourishes for a time and then fades.

All of us know this is true. We know life cannot stand still. Our minds tell us that the admonitions of friends are healthful, but our hearts keep remembering, remembering. . . .

Only when we can give gratitude for the precious things that were ours in bygone days shall we ever be able to hold them close without pain.

~e·e~

Scorn

All who honored her despise her,
. . . .
"Look, O Lord, and behold,
for I am despised." (Lamentations 1:8,11)

"Despised! Of course not," a friend says.

Oh, yes, my friend, we are. Or should I say scorned? Gently but truly scorned. Else why are you uncomfortable in our presence? Why do you appear relieved when your visit is over? But if you think "scorn" is still too harsh a word, then grant us the right to maintain that we are an embarrassment. On this point, although C.S. Lewis is speaking as a widower, his words fit a widow too. After the death of his wife, he wrote:

I cannot talk to the children about her. The moment I try, there appears on their faces neither grief, nor love, nor fear, nor pity, but the most fatal of all nonconductors, embarrassment.

It isn't only the boys either. An odd byproduct of my loss is that I'm aware of being an embarrassment to everyone I meet. At work, at the club, in the street. . . . Perhaps the bereaved ought to be isolated in special settlements like lepers. . . .

To some I'm worse than an embarrassment. I am as a death's head. Wherever I meet a happily married pair, I can feel them both thinking, "One or the other of us must someday be as he is now."[6]

~e·e~

Self-Pity

Little wonder then that for a time we indulge in self-pity. We appropriate for our own use the outcry attributed to Jesus in Stainer's "Crucifixion":

Is it nothing to you,
all you who pass by?
Look and see if there is any sorrow
like my sorrow
which was brought upon me.
(Lamentations 1:12)

In the throes of early widowhood we are certain that no one knows the depth of our grief — no one except perhaps another widow. Then seeing a friend who has been widowed for years and is again living normally, we doubt that even she knows, or ever knew.

When widows think there is no sorrow like their own, they are basically correct. A recent best seller confirms this belief.

In *Future Shock*, the results of a multi-year study covering thousands of people in dozens of countries and varying age and income levels are summarized in the following brief but well-documented conclusion: "The death of a spouse . . .

is almost universally regarded as the single most impactful change that can befall a person in the normal course of his life."[7]

In the verses above we have seen ourselves as wailers. Now we see ourselves plagued with

<e·e>

Self-Incrimination

**My transgressions were bound
into a yoke;
by his hand they were fastened
together;
they were set upon my neck.**

(Lamentations 1:14)

Transgressions! All our sins of commission and sins of omission come to plague us. What was it I did or failed to do? Maybe if I had been more careful about his diet. If only I had relieved him from tensions, spent more time with him relaxing, gone to that conference with him, made him stay home from that last city council meeting. If only I had done this. If only I hadn't done that. . . . A thousand "if only's" bundled into a yoke are set upon the neck like the fateful albatross.

Daphne du Maurier records that following the first bewildered fit of weeping after the death of her husband, she began to blame herself. "I could have done more," she laments, "observed with sharp awareness the ominous signs . . . . sat with him all night"[8] that last night. That last night! Whoever knows what night is going to be the last night?

In like manner Clarissa Start yearns to relive that last day. The day before her husband died, he had come to the door of her study, half-stating, half-asking, "Oh, you're busy?"

"Yes, terribly busy," she had answered, typing away to meet a deadline.

Now she laments, "Why wasn't I a better wife?"[9]

This is a universal cry. Who among us widows does not sometime or other, over some circumstance or other, cry, "Why wasn't I a better wife?" And if the husband be left a widower, does he not also at times lament, "Why wasn't I a better husband?" Having regrets is the price of being human — and perhaps the true measure of our love.

But no widow, no widower is fair to herself/himself if the final judgment of the goodness of the relationship to the beloved is based only upon the "last word" or the activities of the "last day." Not unless the sum total of all words said, of all deeds done before that "last hour" had been bad should one deplete life with the barren, unprofitable cry, "Why wasn't I better?"

Yet for all our post-rationalizations, regrets will come, self-incriminations will rise to torment us, self-pity will grow large, tears will flow, feelings of being despised will not be downed. All are an inevitable part of the syndrome of early grief.

Emotional Numbers

Emotional Numbers

Can numbers raise your blood pressure, rouse jealousy, send you to depths of despair, turn you into a recluse, and then, by an aberration of new math, form themselves into a strange problem in old math division?

The problem:

$$\frac{2 \ + \ \frac{1}{2} \ + \ 5th}{10,000,000} = \ ?$$

No use programming these numbers through a computer. The mechanical brain that could handle them has not yet been invented, nor may it ever be. It takes a human brain, a pulsing heart, a manageable will, and an elusive something else to deal with emotional numbers.

And that is what 2, ½, 5, and 10,000,000 are: four emotional numbers making one highly perplexing fraction. Or, to be precise, they are the numbers that produce explosive emotions.

The number "2" is for couples: the starry-eyed boy-girl couple walking the streets and parks arm-in-arm, and the man-woman couple entering their own home for the first time, she being carried in his arms over the threshold, then in the morning and through the years following coming out together, secure in their love for each other. Each twosome finds being a couple "the nicest thing in the world." Affection, love, passion — what richer gifts has life to offer?

Vicki and Bill were one of these couples. I met them at church five years ago on the Sunday before Thanksgiving. During the singing of the hymns Bill's rich baritone rose above all other voices. When we came to the Doxology:

Praise God from whom all blessings flow;
Praise Him all creatures here below;
Praise Him above, ye heavenly host;
Praise Father, Son, and Holy Ghost,

I felt that if I received no more from that service than his singing I would be doubly blessed.

After the service I learned they had been shopping around for a church. Now they had decided they liked this church best. When I suggested he sing in the choir, Bill put his arm about Vicki, drawing her close, and said, "Couldn't do that. Couldn't leave my bride alone."

"You see," she said, "I don't sing. Can't carry a tune. Bill has to sing for both of us."

"And I like to be near her when I sing," said Bill.

As the months went by, from time to time Vicki shared memories with me and kept me posted on their activities.

They had collided in a January snowstorm the year they were both seniors at an eastern college. From then on, they lived in a dream world. They knew almost immediately that they were "made for each other." After their marriage in June, they moved across country to Oregon. Bill was to teach in a high school. They rented the first modest ranch-style house in a new suburban division, and they didn't mind having no neighbors. They were happy and content in their own togetherness, finding ever increasing joy in being a "married couple."

"The twain shall be one," Bill said, swinging Vicki around until her feet left the floor. "Preacher knew what he was talking about."

Then one day a couple moved into the new house next door, and a few days later another couple moved into the house on the other side and a couple into the house across the street. Within a week the four couples were getting to know each other and finding they had much in common, the most significant being the proximity of their wedding dates. All had been married in June.

Every week they met for bridge, and every week the hostess tried to outdo the hostess of the previous week. The men said, "So good once a week to have a dessert loaded with calories!" and everybody laughed. The eight of them laughed a great deal, sometimes over the simplest of things. It was fun meeting together, sharing experiences, recipes, jokes, plans, games. Just the eight of them. Four cozy couples. There wasn't room for anyone else.

A year later, on a day in June that they all decided upon as a compromise mutual wedding date, Bess and Chuck entertained. "A first wedding anniversary party," Bess said. And party it was, indeed, formal with all the trimmings. A gourmet feast served at Bess's beautifully appointed table that seated eight comfortably but never any more, with women and men properly spaced.

As the years went by, first one, then another of the couples moved from the area, but never were they too distant from each other to prevent their meeting together. After the second wedding anniversary, they met twice a month instead of every week, and after their fourth anniversary they decided to meet only once a month. All except Vicki and Bill had young children, and all the husbands and wives had become involved in many other activities. None, however, took precedence over those monthly meetings of "The Couples."

By rotation, their joint fifth wedding anniversary was held at Bess and Chuck's house. During dessert, Vicki, her blue eyes sparkling, said, "Isn't it wonderful how we four couples have stayed together! One of these days we may not be close enough to meet as we have these last five years, but I make a motion now that we all meet for our twenty-fifth! No matter where we are, let's come together for that, even if we have to come from the ends of the earth!"

"Even from outer space," Bill added. Everybody laughed and promised.

On the way home Vicki moved close to Bill, laid her head on his shoulder, and drew a long breath. "Oh, Bill, I'm so lucky being married to you. Nobody could ever be happier than I am!"

"I'm pretty lucky myself." Bill drew her closer. "Being a married couple is something very special."

"Together forever and ever," Vicki murmured.

But forever was not to be. The next day while on his way to work, Bill became the victim of a hit-and-run driver. The news of his death took all of four lines in the daily paper.

Now, during Vicki's fresh grief, I visited her frequently. A month after the accident I found her at her kitchen table, a slim volume of poetry in her hand. It was late morning, yet her breakfast dishes were still on the table.

"Read this," she said, handing me the book. "I had no idea other people feel as I do until I found this."

The book was open at a poem headed "Couples." It began

I hate couples, men and women, old,
Or young or in-between. The paired, I
  hold
As personal affront.[1]

Down the page was a long list of couples: on country roads, in restaurants, on planes or trains or ships. . . . Couples reading a book together, listening to music, or gardening, going to bed together and rising again!

"She hates them all," Vicki said. "So do I. I even hate the word 'couple.'" When I looked up, I saw hardness in her face, a grim set to her mouth.

"I can't bear to see couples walking arm-in-arm, driving out in a car together, sitting in church, his arm over the back of the seat and she nestling close. It's all I can do not to scream at them." Vicki paused. Then, "But what could I say? Surely not 'You make me so jealous!' But they do. Violently jealous. And that's wrong for me to feel that way. I should remember how it was for Bill and me. I should be glad for them, but I'm not. I'm hurting with envy."

I nodded. I knew how she felt. It takes a long time to control that particular violent emotion. It was good, though, to hear Vicki say, "I should remember. . . ." That showed that she was reaching out for the only weapon capable of dealing with jealousy — being glad for another's joy. But handling that weapon takes much practice.

For a short time neither of us spoke. On the kitchen shelf the old wind-up clock that Bill had bought at a rummage sale ticked away the minutes.

Vicki reached over and plugged in the coffee pot. "Well," she said, wiping her eyes, "I could at least offer a cup of coffee, something to dilute the sob stuff I've just been serving. I'm ashamed of being so jealous. Believe me, I really am."

"I believe. Go on. Talk. It's good for you."

She gave me a sharp look as though measuring my sincerity. Then, "Okay. Since I've spilled so much already I may as well spill the rest. It's this terrible, terrible feeling I have of being bisected, being cut in two. I feel I'm just half a person. It's a strange, frightening feel-ing. I haven't mentioned it to anyone. They'd think I'm going nuts. But," eager for my understanding, "you don't, do you?"

"No, indeed. It's a common feeling for widows. One of us has said that she felt at times as if she had been rudely cut down the middle by a buzz saw. 'Only half of me was left.'"[2]

"But why should I?" Vicki asked. "I was a whole person before I married Bill. Why should I feel like only half a person now?"

"Because," I sought for words, "— because you are half an integer, half of the 'one' you became when the minister said, 'And the twain shall be one flesh.' Remember when he said that?"

Now it was Vicki's turn to nod. All her life she would remember, and I knew that for a long, long time she would feel maimed. The scar of the incision that makes "one" become "one-half" is infinitely slow in healing.

On my way home I thought, *although a husband may call his wife "the better half," when you're a widow you're "the worse half."* But the adjectives "better" and "worse" are inconsequential. The salient word is "half." That is the fraction that casts a widow into deep despair and leads her into despondency.

The weeks passed and Vicki weathered them better than I first thought she would. Now and then she would pour out her heart, and I would have glimpses

of the battles she had been fighting: what to do with Bill's belongings; coming to the decision not to move yet and not to take anyone in to live with her, even not to go back East to be with her folks for a while until she had everything cleared and straightened up. "Maybe for Christmas. The folks were out for the funeral. It isn't as though I hadn't seen them."

When I called on her in mid-October — it was four months to the day since Bill had been killed — I was dismayed to find her in tears. She had appeared to be, as one friend said, "coming out of it." Like "coming out from ether."

Not a bad simile at that, for grief does call for an anesthetic, and in many cases at the time of initial grief nature appears to release its own special insulation from great pain. Else how could a pioneer mother have lined a small rough coffin for her first-born? Or the young widow of a country's president follow on foot the hearse of her husband?

All of us, seeing Vicki on the day of Bill's funeral, knew she moved in some kind of protective anesthesia, and in the weeks that followed, after the first numbing effect had worn off, it did appear that Vicki, except for her withdrawal from socializing, was "coming through fine."

But now here she was, four months after the funeral, in a well of despair.

Her story came wet with tears. The "old group" had been urging her to come to their monthly get-together, but she hadn't gone. "Just couldn't bear going alone."

"We'll call for you," they said.

"No, no. I can drive myself. It's just —"

They understood. "Of course. Later."

Now four months had passed, and they thought she should bestir herself, stop being a recluse. She ought to get out of the house. Bill would want her to be with old friends again in their homes.

"Well, last week Bess called. 'Vicki, please, please come next Wednesday. It's Chuck's birthday. I'm having a surprise party. Lollie and Jack will bring you.'"

Vicki demurred, but at last she yielded to Bess's urging. When Lollie and Jack came for her, they echoed Bess's words. "Bill would want you to keep up with old friends. You mustn't become a recluse."

"So you see they're all talking about me," Vicki said. "I wish they'd leave me alone." She paused a moment.

"Both Lollie and Jack came to the door," she continued. "Lollie gave me a big hug. When Jack hugged me too, I thought I'd faint. A man's arms around me again — but not Bill's! When we got to the car, Lollie took her place in the front seat and moved over for me to sit beside her, but Jack opened the back door for me."

"'Oh, I thought —' Lollie began. Jack said, 'Too crowded in the front.' Then Lollie got out and came to sit with me in the back."

"Thoughtful of her," I said.

"Very. That's why I feel so terrible about what happened afterwards."

A fresh flow of tears interrupted her. Once again in control, she continued, "I made a fool of myself. When I got there and saw three couples together, I felt tears starting and went to Lollie and whispered, 'Take me home. I want to go home.' By this time I couldn't keep back the tears. Oh, why did I have to cry like that then? I thought I'd cried myself out, but there I was crying even harder than I did at the cemetery four months ago. And here I am crying again. Will tears never dry?"

"They will — in time, but maybe not as soon as you think they will."

The memory of my own flash flood of tears more than two years after Elam's death came again as clear as though it had been only yesterday. I was at White Temple in Portland, Oregon, to give a speech about our years in China as missionaries. We had finished dinner and the leader had come forward to direct fellowship singing. At the first few notes of the piano accompaniment I stiffened. They were the introduction to the Latvian Hymn I had chosen to be sung at Elam's funeral service in Redlands and at the graveside in Orchard Park, New York.

Before the group had finished singing the first line, "My God and I we walk the fields together . . ."[3] a torrent of tears struck me like a hurricane.

Remembering that experience, I touched Vicki's hand and said, "You may find yourself weeping like this two years from now, as I once did. But be patient. Tears are a safety valve."

When her spasm had eased, I asked, "Did you go home?"

"No. After a while I got control of myself. [As I did, too, I remembered, and went on to give the speech that night at White Temple.] But I wish I had gone right then."

"Why?"

"Because later what I did was worse. You know Bess, how she is when she entertains. Everything perfect. At the table there always has to be an equal number of men and women."

"Oh, no," I groaned within myself. "She couldn't have brought in an extra man, not so soon, for Vicki!"

My fear, though, was groundless, for Vicki was saying, "Well, last night Bess didn't seat us all at the table. She seated us at two card tables: three men at one, four women at the other. None of us had ever done that kind of segregating before."

Vicki paused, used a fresh tissue, straightened, and spoke with vehemence, "You sometimes hear about the 'fifth wheel.' Well, let me tell you, there's a world of difference between hearing about a fifth wheel and *being* one!"

"My dear, you don't have to tell me. I know, have known for more than a quarter of a century." Then, "You said you made a fool of yourself. How?"

"As we were eating dessert," Vicki went on with her story, "I mean as the rest were eating — I was too choked up to do more than taste — the doorbell rang. Bess went to the door, and I heard her say, 'No, no. Just old friends. Do come in. I've been hoping you'd come soon.' Then she introduced the visitors to all of us. 'Our new neighbors,' she said. 'Maybe they'll —' Then she stopped. Chuck finished the sentence for her 'play bridge. Now we can have two tables.'

"Bess looked startled and said, 'Oh, I hadn't planned games for tonight. I — I thought we'd just talk or maybe — maybe show pictures. No games.'

"I knew why. There were nine of us, not eight. Before I realized what I was saying, I cried, 'Of course, no games. How could you with a fifth wheel around?' And then the tears came again. It was like a flood breaking a dam. That time I couldn't stop. I stumbled over to Lollie and begged, 'Take me home, take me home.'

"Oh, what can a person do to stop tears like that in a group? They are devastating."

What could I say? Certainly I had had no answer for myself that night at White Temple. There my tears had to run their course, and although over the years I've managed to avoid such an exhibition in a crowd, I have had a few freshets in the presence of one or two friends. I searched my mind — and then I remembered.

"Do what another widow did when this same thing happened to her. Count! Count the flowers on someone's hat."

Distracted, Vicki laughed unsteadily, "But nobody wears hats these days."

"Then count anything. Start counting to 10,000,000."

"Why 10,000,000?" Vicki was startled. "Such an enormous figure. I'd never come to the end."

"No need to finish. Concentrating on the first 100 should help dry your tears."

"But what's that number for?"

"For us widows, Vicki. For the 10,000,000 of us in our country today."

Taking paper and pen from my bag, I set down the aberrant problem and handed the paper to her.

$$\frac{2 \; + \; \frac{1}{2} \; + \; 5th}{10,000,000} = \; ?$$

"Does this mean anything to you, Vicki?"

She studied it for a minute. Then with a wan smile she said, "I never was good at division, but I'll make a guess.

"We are not alone."[4]

The Sympathizing Thought

The Sympathizing Thought

For several days, Vicki's plea, "Oh, what can a person do to stop tears like that?" kept echoing. She meant, I knew, tears in public and before a group. In private or with an understanding friend, she would weep, should weep, for tears are a safety valve, a gift from God.

In time, though, even in these two situations she would have to come to exercise restraint. Like other God-given gifts — the senses and the appetites: muscular, gustatory, sexual — tears, too, are subject to control. Undisciplined, they can become pathological.

The suggestion I gave Vicki is merely a stopgap. Counting numbers, swift and diverting as that help may be, is too mechanical, too impersonal. Besides, to her the number 10,000,000 is enormous, and I am certain, as it is to me, also benumbing and overwhelming. Her answer to the problem in division, "We are not alone," implied empathy. But how effectively can one empathize *en masse*?

Wouldn't specific names be more helpful than impersonal numbers — say names of other widows? But they must be names of persons far enough removed from her so that they would evoke only a sympathizing thought, not "the sympathizing tear." Tears were what she wanted to control.

The question then: What rosters to draw her gently within the circle of comfort and strength that comes from knowing one is not alone?

Suggestions came freewheeling: widows of the Bible, widows of literature, widows among the Mothers of the Year, widows in business, widows — yes, widows of the White House.

Two years ago in the Library of Congress I took notes for a speech about those widows. A search uncovered my notes in a box labeled "To be sorted."

Impulsively I reached for the phone. "Hello, Vicki? Hope you haven't started supper."

"Supper? Is it that late already?"

"Good. Then you haven't. So how about coming over here?"

"I'd love to. This eating alone isn't —"

"Isn't easy," I finished for her. "Not at all easy."

A jet of memory whisked me back twenty-eight years to my first meal alone at Claremont Inn, the quiet, quaint inn set among towering eucalyptus trees — a place Elam and I had regarded as quite special. Now I stood at the entrance alone waiting for the hostess. All of me wanted to turn and run away, but I was rooted to the spot. No strength left to run, hardly strength to stand. Not a human being at all, but a terrified animal at bay, spent from the chase, encamped about by the host of loneliness.

"Hello. Hello. Are you there?" Vicki's voice called me back to the present.

"Yes. Yes, I'm here. Supper tonight. Six, or would seven be better for you?"

"No difference to me. All hours are the same these days."

"Then make it six."

Later, dessert finished, I told her of my afternoon thoughts. "Widows and places by names, not just numbers. Let's start with the Bible."

She remembered the importunate widow of the parable. "The persistent female who wore down the judge. Hand me the concordance, please, so I can find the passage."

Having found it, she read aloud:

And he told them a parable, to the effect that they ought always to pray and not lose heart. He said, "In a certain city there was a judge who neither feared God nor regarded man; and there was a widow in that city who kept coming to him and saying, 'Vindicate me against my adversary.' For a while he refused; but afterward he said to himself, 'Though I neither fear God nor regard man, yet because this widow bothers me, I will vindicate her, or she will wear me out by her continual coming.'" And the Lord said, "Hear what the unrighteous judge says. And will not God vindicate his elect, who cry to him day and night? Will he delay long over them? I tell you, he will vindicate them speedily. Nevertheless, when the Son of man comes, will he find faith on earth?"

(Luke 18:1-8)

When she finished, she mused, "Will he find such faith in me?"

"Or in me?" I echoed.

Both of us hoped he would.

Now it was my turn. I chose the story of the widow who gave the mite.

And he sat down opposite the treasury, and watched the multitude putting money into the treasury. Many rich people put in large sums. And a poor widow came, and put in two copper coins, which make a penny. And he called his disciples to him, and said to them, "Truly, I say to you, this poor widow

has put in more than all those who are contributing to the treasury. For they all contributed out of their abundance; but she out of her poverty has put in everything she had, her whole living."
(Mark 12:41-44)

"And to think, " Vicki said, "that out of all the people Jesus saw that day, among them the rich putting in large sums, only this poor widow and her two copper coins won his praise!"

The widow of Nain came to my mind next, but, in deference to Vicki's having no children, I refrained from mentioning her. Vicki, however, was remembering her too, and she thumbed through the Gospel of Luke until she found the story.

Soon afterward he went to a city called Nain, and his disciples and a great crowd went with him. As he drew near to the gate of the city, behold, a man who had died was being carried out, the only son of his mother, and she was a widow; and a large crowd from the city was with her. And when the Lord saw her, he had compassion on her and said to her, "Do not weep." And he came and touched the bier, and the bearers stood still. And he said, "Young man, I say to you, arise." And the dead man sat up, and began to speak. And he gave him to his mother.
(Luke 7:11-15)

Vicki's gaze remained upon the page. Finally she said, "His first raising of the dead was to comfort a widow. He must have known the depth of her grief. Oh, those words, 'Do not weep'!" A pause, and then, "She had no need to weep. Her dead was given back to her. What if the lad had remained dead?"

For moments she said nothing more, but I knew that her heart was crying, "Why, oh why could it not have been like that for me?" The eternal "Why?" of all who mourn.

In the time of quietness I went to the bookcase and brought back a copy of *Jesus and Woman*. "Here," I said, "is a chapter on the 'Widow of Nain.' Years ago I marked these passages."

She is not the only widow we meet in the Gospels. Jesus seems to have let His eyes often linger upon them, and always in chivalry and understanding. . . . A widow knows that it was not flesh alone which bound her to her husband, but the delight of mind working on mind, of spirit growing into spirit; she is like a creature cut in two, when he is gone.[1]

"Let me see that." Vicki reached for the book, looked at the copyright date, and exclaimed, "Incredible that a woman writing in 1946, the year I was born, should have felt that half-a-person too!"

"Why incredible? Lady Hosie was a widow when she wrote the book. She wrote from experience. Widowhood transcends time and space and nationality."

Returning to the Bible, we thought of two widows in the Old Testament linked by a singularly common experience. Both Elijah and Elisha helped and were helped by widows.

Then the word of the Lord came to him [Elijah], "Arise, go to Zarephath, which belongs to Sidon, and dwell there. Behold, I have commanded a widow there to feed you."

(1 Kings 17:8, 9)

Again, out of consideration for Vicki, I stopped there. Why expand on another story that had to do with a son?

"But that's not the end," she said. "I know the rest. The woman had a son, and he became very sick. 'No breath left in him.' And Elijah stretched himself upon the boy and cried to the Lord, and the Lord heard him and life came back, and Elijah gave the boy to his mother. That was the widow who had only a handful of meal and a little oil in a cruse when Elijah asked for food."

The jar of meal that was not spent and the cruse of oil that did not fail! A quick, silent prayer went up from my heart, "Oh, Lord, Vicki's jar of courage, her cruse of joy so depleted! Fill them both again."

"And that story about Elisha," Vicki was saying. "It's something like this one about Elijah. A widow there, too, and oil."

And children, I thought, but Vicki wanted the story.

"Read it aloud," she said.
So I read:

Now the wife of one of the sons of the prophets cried to Elisha, "Your servant my husband is dead; and you know that your servant feared the Lord, but the creditor has come to take my two children to be his slaves." And Elisha said to her, "What shall I do for you? Tell me; what have you in the house?" And she said, "Your maidservant has nothing in the house, except a jar of oil." Then he said, "Go outside, borrow vessels of all your neighbors, empty vessels and not too few. Then go in, and shut the door upon yourself and your sons, and pour into all these vessels; and when one is full, set it aside." So she went from him and shut the door upon herself and her sons; and as she poured they brought the vessels to her. When the vessels were full, she said to her son, "Bring me another vessel." And he said to her, "There is not another." Then the oil stopped flowing. She came and told the man of God, and he said, "Go, sell the oil and pay your debts, and you and your sons can live on the rest."

(2 Kings 4:1-7)

Again a jar of oil. This one not only did not fail of itself, but was the source for filling many other jars.

To my earlier prayer I added another. "Lord, help her find some new growing edge of life: some 'oil of joy for mourning.' And let the oil be enough to fill other empty lives." Helping others, I knew, was one shortcut to comfort.

For a time there was no sound but that of the rush of traffic on the highway. Busy, active life passing us by. . . .

Then, breaking through, came the evening hymn from the college chimes nearby.

Lead, kindly Light, amid the encircling gloom,
Lead Thou me on!

• • • • • • • • • • • • • • • • • • •

And with the morn those angel faces smile,
Which I have loved long since, and lost a-while.

When the last bell tone was gone, Vicki reached over and touched me lightly. "You do believe, don't you, that there's life after death; that we will see those we've lost awhile?" The pleading in her voice was pathetic.

"With all my heart I believe that. How could I not believe with Jesus' own words to assure me?"

"Let not your hearts be troubled; believe in God, believe also in me. In my Father's house are many rooms; if it were not so, would I have told you that I go to prepare a place for you? And when I go and prepare a place for you, I will come again and will take you to myself, that where I am you may be also."

(John 14:1-3)

"Now —" I stood up, breaking the spell that was upon us. "Now let me introduce you to the widows of the White House." I brought over the folder of notes from my desk, took out one sheet and gave it to Vicki. "Here's a roster for you. When tears threaten to overflow in public, remembering that widowhood is no respecter of persons may help to check them."

I watched her gaze move over the names and dates and figures:

Name	Term as First Lady	Years of Widowhood
Anna Harrison	(March 4 - April 4, 1841)	20
Margaret Taylor	(1849-1850)	2
Mary Todd Lincoln*	(1861-1865)	17
Lucretia Garfield*	(March 4 - Sept. 19, 1881)	37
Ida McKinley*	(1897-1901)	6
Florence Harding	(1921-1923)	1
Eleanor Roosevelt	(1933-1945)	17
Jacqueline Kennedy*	(1961-1963)	Remarried

*Made a widow by an assassin's bullet

When she had taken in all the items, she looked up. "Strange," she said, "I've never thought of any of these as widows, except Jackie. But even in 1963 'widow' didn't mean to me what it means now.

"Look at Anna Harrison. Only one month in the White House when her husband died!"

"Maybe not even that long. One account I read stated she never did live there. On the day of the Inauguration she was too ill to attend, and she was still too ill to move there during the fatal cold that her husband caught from insisting upon going hatless and coatless on that day. He died a month later."

"Leaving Anna," Vicki's words came singly, wrapped in sympathy, "to live through twenty years alone. Stubborn, willful man! However did she manage?"

"Mainly through the comfort of her church and her children — ten of them."

"Twenty years of widowhood for her. Only two for Margaret Taylor." Vicki was following the roster. "But Margaret had a longer time as First Lady of the White House than Anna had. Was it a full year?"

"Sixteen months, my notes say. But she was not at all happy being there. She was a homebody and would have much preferred keeping house in private to hostessing the social whirl of the White House. In a way, though, she succeeded when, because of her health, she turned over official entertaining to her daughter Betty."

"One would think that after forty years of hard living in the pioneer military posts where her husband had been stationed, she deserved 'a little gray home in the West'; instead, she got the White House in Washington, D.C."

"Quite different from Mary Todd Lincoln, wasn't she?" Vicki said. "Mary wanted to reign in the White House. At least so she was presented in 'The Lincoln Mask' that I saw recently."

"Yes," I said, "from all I have read about her, I would say she was ambitious for that position. And she had it for four years."

"Then on that tragic Good Friday night she lost it." Vicki knew the story well from the play she had seen. "I wonder how many times she thought or said, 'If only I hadn't insisted that he go with me to the theater that night.'"

"If only —" "If only —" "If only —" The words toll like a dirge through many widowhoods.

"Regrets? Yes, I'm sure she must have had them," I said. "Who doesn't? But few widows have the deep mental agony she had during her seventeen years alone. Remember how, after a jury pronounced her insane, she attempted suicide? Among the White House widows I think she was the most pathetic."

"More so than Lucretia Garfield with thirty-seven years of being alone?" Vicki asked.

"Yes, I think so, for in addition to mental agony, Mary Todd lacked the financial easement that Congress granted to Lucretia."

"But thirty-seven years!" Vicki saw only that figure. "Why, that's a longer time than I've lived! However could she endure thirty-seven years?"

I waited for Vicki's attention, then caught it full force when I said, "A few days before President McKinley was assassinated I was among a small crowd gathered to see him at a whistle stop close to my home in Buffalo, New York."

"You're kidding." Her look of incredulity amused me. "Goodness that was way back in 1901."

"Ancient history," I said. "Yes, I know, but I did see him and hear him. He spoke from the rear platform of his private car.

"More exciting than that, though, was having Mrs. McKinley smile at me through the window of the dining car — or was it the parlor car? She was sitting at a table on which there was a large basket of the most luscious fruit I had ever seen.

"I raced home to tell my mother and father, 'She smiled at me! She smiled at me!' To myself I thought, *Something to tell my grandchildren*. And I at that time only ten!

"A few days later the news came: President McKinley Shot! Along with neighbors up and down our street and across the nation, we draped our house in black. But my sadness was not so much for the President as for his wife — his widow now. My first awareness of the sorrow of widowhood came at that time. What would the lovely lady do without her big, strong husband?

"Florence Harding's sorrow brought no such reaction. There was no personal relationship with her."

"I," said Vicki, "am glad to see that Mrs. Harding lived only one year after her husband died. That's even too long to live alone."

"Vicki!" The reprimand in my tone startled her — and me. "How can you say that? Think of the millions of women who have never married and live alone and yet live a good life — good for themselves and good for others.

"Would you have had Eleanor Roosevelt live for less than a year after President Roosevelt died? Look at all she did in those seventeen years of her widowhood. In those years she carved out a life of her own that was without precedent.

"In April, 1865, Mary Todd Lincoln began her seventeen years alone shrouding herself in self-pity and ego lamentation. Eighty years later in another April, Eleanor Roosevelt began her seventeen years alone donning a cape of compassion ample enough to enfold hundreds of persons of differing races and creeds.

"Let me recall for you what she did in those seventeen years alone. She was the first woman delegate to the United Nations General Assembly and the United States representative to the Human Rights Commission. She wrote books and a syndicated newspaper column. She spoke from platforms across our country and the world. And in her busy public life she still had time for countless deeds of friendly personal concern.

"I'll never forget the time in Redlands when I was privileged to have her as honored guest for an afternoon reception and a buffet supper in our home. It was that spring when the golden poppies and blue lupin were especially abundant. During a lull in the reception line when she told me she had been in Bakersfield, I said, 'Oh, then you must have seen the wildflowers. Wonderfully beautiful this year, aren't they?'

"'Wildflowers? No, I saw no wildflowers. I went to see the migrant workers there.'

"Now, Vicki, you wouldn't think a year too long for a widow like Eleanor Roosevelt, would you?"

"No, of course. You win. But then Mrs. Roosevelt was exceptional."

"True. But some of the others were also exceptional — each in her own way. Think of Jacqueline Kennedy."

"Oh, Jackie! I can't think of her without tears. The first thing that comes to my mind is seeing her on television, standing with her children as the casket went by and young John at her side saluting. The most poignant sight I've ever witnessed."

From there we went on speaking of Jackie in other situations — of her and of others until the evening grew close to midnight.

The next Sunday afternoon my phone rang. A friend asked in a worried tone, "What's happened to Vicki?"

"What do you mean 'happened'?" I asked.

"Well, I sat next to her in church this morning, and during the Doxology she kept saying to herself, 'Nain, Anna, Lucretia, Mary, Eleanor.'"

"Was she crying?"

"No, she was just saying those words over and over."

"Glory be!" I exclaimed, close to a shout.

The Special Days

The Special Days

Even though Vicki had said, "I'll remember," and had demonstrated on Sunday morning two weeks ago that she had and was gaining control over impending tears, she still had battles to face. One dark confrontation loomed up now — Bill's birthday, the day before Thanksgiving.

"How can I get through that day?" Her cry was a wail. "And then the next day and soon Christmas." She paused. "And after that our special day in January."

I knew about that special January date, the day she and Bill had collided in a snowstorm on an eastern college campus, the day their romance began. Hardest of all days would be this first special one without Bill. They had always made so much of it. If snow hadn't fallen yet here in the Willamette Valley, they had gone to Mt. Hood or Mt. Rainier where they were sure to find even deeper snow than they had had in the East.

"What will I do? How will I get through these special days?" She sat staring out the window. The last oak leaves from her neighbor's tree were being buffeted around by a strong wind, but one could tell she was seeing none of them. My heart ached for her.

After a while she turned to face me and put the question directly and personally, "How did you get through?"

How did I get through? The question startled me. Those first special days without Elam — how far away they now were! A quarter of a century away. But Vicki's question brought them near.

Years ago I wrote letters about those days and had them printed in a booklet *When Death Steps In*,[1] now out of print. I wondered if I even had a copy left; months ago I'd loaned my own last copy to a friend. Had she returned it? I couldn't remember.

"Wait," I said to Vicki. "Maybe — just maybe I can find what I want."

At home I found the returned copy in

a box marked "For filing." I took it to Vicki and said, "Here in the eighth and ninth letters you'll find at least a partial answer to your question. Read them for yourself. We'll talk about them later."

This One Thing More

And now comes Thanksgiving — your first Season of Thanks with an empty chair in your home. All around you voices are praising God and saying:

Bless the Lord, O my soul,
And forget not all His benefits.

But you cannot sing; your heart is too heavy.

I know how you feel, although for me the struggle with gratitude did not come at my first Thanksgiving after Death stepped in, but some months later. Not until a certain day in spring, a day that had been a private thanksgiving day for Elam and me, did my real test come.

At the time I was in a period of depression. It was not that I had lost my faith in continuing life nor my assurance that we would meet again. My faith continued to be a strong anchor, but it was anchoring me only to the future. What I needed was something to hold me to the past. I needed the comfort of memories, but that comfort was being denied because now for a period I had been able to think

of the past only with regret and sorrow that it was so soon over. Take, for instance, the anniversary date that was fast approaching. Memories of how it had been in other years brought a longing so intense it was like a physical ache. The "dark night of the soul" was definitely upon me.

Our special day fell on a Sunday that year. My mother and my younger son left home early to go to choir rehearsal before church. At first I thought that I would not go to church, but the habit of the years prevailed and I went — alone, of course. For some reason no friend came to sit with me as friends had been doing.

I dutifully followed the service, but little of it reached me. I felt sure that I could not stay to the end. While the ushers were walking up the aisle, I decided I would slip out after the offering.

The next minute the minister was saying, "Let us pray." I bowed my head. His prayer was simple and short.

Among Thy many other blessings, Lord, grant us now this one thing more — the gift of gratitude.

Never had I heard a prayer so short. Seldom have I known a prayer so swiftly answered.

I have tried several times to put the experience of that moment into words, but I have never been able to do so, and I cannot hope to do so now. All I can say is that some tension within me broke, and all the yesterdays that matched the date came tumbling about me like jewels spilling from a treasure-box. I picked them up and hugged them to me. It was the first time since August that I had actually opened my heart to the past and pressed it close.

Quite spontaneously I prayed in silence, "I thank Thee for this day and for all it has meant through the years." Then I immediately added, "And now, especially, I thank Thee for the gift of gratitude."

With that a miracle happened. The bitterness left me, and in its place came the oil of joy, "beauty for ashes."

To say that since that experience I have not been lonely would be to tell an untruth. The missing is still with me, and I know it will be with me all through life. But the longing now is like the ring on my finger — something to cherish, a token of promise against the day of our meeting again.

Ever since that Sunday, I have used a variation of that same simple prayer for my friends who mourn. I pray it now for you:

Among Thy other comforts, Lord, grant to those who freshly mourn this one comfort more — the gift of gratitude.

The First Christmas After

And after Thanksgiving comes Christmas, your first Christmas after Death has disarranged the pattern of your life. You are dreading its approach. You wish you could skip the season, but the world will not let you. Stores, schools, your friends' homes, churches, radio, television — the very air is full of Christmas. Tinsel, holly, bells, carols everywhere.

I know what you are going through. One intensely dark time for me came as I was struggling with the decision of whether or not to send out greetings. For twenty-five years, ever since our Chinese friends on the mission field had given us the name of *An* (meaning *peace*), I had made the cards for the House of An. But now with Elam not here to sign them with me, how could I alone send greetings from the House?

The conflict was taut with emotion. In the end tradition won, and greetings were sent as usual. With them went this message:

The first two lines of this year's greeting came to me last Christmas. Elam liked them. After August I thought I could not finish the greeting, but a few days ago the poem finished itself. I felt Elam's approval of the last two lines as

---

clearly as I heard his approval of the first two.

The verses for that year are given here in the hope that the comfort of the deepened insight which prompted the writing of them may now be your comfort too.

What power in the Christ-child lay
  To lead three kings afar;
  To cause the angels' song to leap
  Earth's farthest frontier bar;
  With baby hands on heaven's face,
  To halt the morning star!

What power still in Christ-child lies
  To dry earth's bitter tears;
  To keep the Song of Peace alive
  Through weary, war-torn years;
  With pierced hands on aching heart,
  To heal one's deepest fears!

What power yet for future days
  To free the struggling soul;
  To guide slow steps up rugged paths
  Toward distant, shining goal;
  To prove that Here and There are halves
  Of God's eternal Whole!

Three years later the greetings centered about An-di-fan (Chinese for "Place of Peace"), our cabin in the woods. The wish that year was in two parts, which I now renew for you:

May you who love and still have your dear ones near find many happy moments to turn into precious memories.

May you who have loved and lost awhile use your precious memories to make happy moments.

Memories of An-di-fan
(To Elam)

We drank deep draughts from
    forest trees;
(Each dogwood bloom a cup of four.)
We clapped our hands with poplar
    leaves,
And in a cove on moss-grown floor
We bent our knees
Where maples arch to form a
    chapel door.
  Then down the homing aisle of
    evergreens we'd walk,
  Our hearts too full for common talk.

And once, above a fir's tall spire
Upon the Christ-child's night,
We heard the song of angel choir
And saw a shining — sudden, bright;
With hearts on fire
We mounted then the silver streaming
    light
  And for a moment stood where now
    you wait for me —
Upon the threshold of eternity.

While I was still searching for a last word to say to you, the mailman brought the annual Christmas message from our friends the Hansens. The greater part of the letter was given over to seven-year-old Christina's account of the family's summer trip. As I read the fresh and charming account, quiet pleasure filled me.

Then I found myself staring at these words:

Betsy [Christina's sister] is our bad news. We went to Napa one Saturday for a picnic. We found a place in Paradise Park. Suddenly a branch fell. Everybody ran. There wasn't much time to run though. The branch fell on Betsy's head. There was a Lodge nearby so we ran up to the Lodge with Betsy. We found out Betsy was dead. I couldn't believe it. We all cry sometimes — Mother and Daddy and me and other people.

Through my own tears I read the last short paragraph:

We are going to decorate our tree by painting fruit juice cans and hanging them on our tree. We are looking forward to sending your cards and packages to you.

Here now is my last word to help you on your Road to Bethlehem. Christina has said it for me, and because she is so much closer in age to the Babe than any of us, it is as though he himself were saying it:

Decorate your tree. Look forward to sending.

The upward look! The outward reach! They were both his. Only as you and I make them ours can we find again, renewed, the comfort of his birthday's joy.

The Thin Veil

The Thin Veil

Vicki's phone call that night both pleased and puzzled me. "I've read the letters. Thank you for them. They were what I need — 'spoke to my condition,' as the Quakers say. Now I'd like to see all of the veil."

"Veil? What veil?"

"The rest of something in your handwriting. I found one page between two pages of the book of letters. Scribbled on top is 'The Veil Between.' Where's the rest of it? Don't tell me that's all you wrote."

No, it wasn't all. In my files I found a rough draft, minus the first page. How that page found its way into the letters on death, I'll never know. The page was to have been part of a mimeographed booklet that my church had planned last Easter. A number of us who had experienced the death of a dear one had been asked to write "Thoughts on Life After Death." I'd chosen to write from the point of view of a widow. The plan never came to fruition. Yet here was Vicki now wanting to see all of it.

"Not until I clean up the rough draft," I said. "Give me a few days."

The Sunday after Thanksgiving I gave Vicki a copy, now for the first time in print here.

The Thin Veil

Who first said, "The space between a president and a vice-president is only a breath," I do not know, but all of us testify to that truth as we recall the black moment of November, 1963, in Dallas, Texas.

That last breath is most shocking when it comes of a sudden, with no warning whatsoever. Then, much more than when it comes after a lingering illness, it brings into sharp focus how thin indeed the line between life and death. One second, a friend, a relative, a spouse is alive — active, mobile, vivacious, sensitive to the world about, laughing, talking; the next second, dead — lifeless, inert, robbed of all five senses — and silent, oh, so silent!

"He's gone!" Helen cries. That morning at 8:00 he had kissed her good-by and said, "Meet me at 5:00." Before noon she is called to come to the hospital where he had been taken after his heart attack at the office. Before he reached the hospital he died. Over and over Helen cries, "He's gone! He's gone! How can it be? He was so well this morning."

A neighbor, not yet forty, is ready for the long-planned family trip across the country. The trailer and new station wagon are parked. The three children are belted into their seats. The wife pauses to say good-by to her neighbor. The husband takes the driver's seat, honks the horn, and calls, "Come on. We're ready to go." When she comes, he has already "gone."

A renowned professor, who a few years ago retired to his dream home in Greece, is invited to return to his university for special honors. He and his wife fly to Boston. They are nearing their journey's end, excited about the coming celebration. "I never thought —" he says. The rest is lost in the announcement, "You may now unfasten your seat belts." The wife unfastens hers. The professor emeritus makes no move to unfasten his. "Oh, but it can't be!" the new widow cries — widow before she has yet realized that she is a widow. "Just this minute he was speaking to me!"

Reports of sudden deaths are legion. They bring us up short before the "thin veil." "Last bridge," "bend in the road," "ocean bar," "thin veil" — many expressions are used to define that narrow No Man's Land between life and death. All the terms are open-ended, suggesting continuing existence beyond the veil, the bend, the bridge, the bar.

We are well aware, of course, that not all persons subscribe to this implication. Some persons call it "wishful thinking," so certain are they that there is no life after death. "When a person is dead, he's dead," say these non-believers.

Even without supporting statistics, though, it seems fair to say that these persons form a small minority of the world's population, for east and west, north and south, on land and on islands in the seven seas, sacrifices and chants, potions and prayers, candles and litanies testify to a wide-spread belief in some form of life continuing after death.

About that "life beyond" there exist a variety of conjectures. Non-Christian religions are full of them, some in vivid detail. Even among Christians, where resurrection from the dead is a primary factor of faith, beliefs vary, each documented by Scripture. Some believers say we wait before we enter the blessed state.

"But in those days, after the tribulation, the sun will be darkened, and the moon will not give its light, and the stars will be falling from heaven, and the powers in the heaven will be shaken. And then they will see the Son of man coming in clouds with great power and glory. And then he will send out the angels, and gather his elect from the four winds, from the ends of the earth to the ends of heaven.

(Mark 13:24-27)

Others say, "Not so. We shall straightway be transported." These base their belief on Jesus' word to the criminal on the cross beside him who said,

"Jesus, remember me when you come into your kingdom." And he said to him, "Truly, I say to you, today you will be with me in Paradise."

(Luke 23:42, 43)

One says, "It will be a time of rest. In that sweet by-and-by there will be no labor, no sweat, no tears." Another says, "I'd be bored just sitting with folded hands — or will it be wings?" This one never tires of telling the old story of the soul on the other side of death who, after sumptuous meals and rollicking entertainment, asked for some work. "Something to do. Anything. This vacation atmosphere is killing me. I'd rather be in hell than here." "Where," asked the custodian of the work-less place, "do you think you are?"

But in spite of differences, all Christians have the uncomplicated, direct promise of Jesus:

"In my Father's house are many rooms; if it were not so, would I have told you that I go to prepare a place for you? And when I go and prepare a place for you, I will come again and will take you to myself, that where I am you may be also."

(John 14:2-4)

These simple words imply a continuation of the ego, the entity that we possess here in mortal life. The *I* and *you* of Here will remain the same *I* and the same *you* There.

Elizabeth Yates accepts this as axiomatic.

A plummeting time comes for me when I let myself wonder if I shall ever see him again, as I knew him. My immediate need is for "Yes," but the stark answer that I must give myself is "No." Were I to meet today some friend of my childhood days, or of my school years, neither one would look now as he did then. Yet, no matter what time might have done to us, we would recognize each other. They have been growing and changing as I have, and yet the qualities that first drew us together will be there: stronger, clearer, more radiant than in the early days.[1]

Today, as always, we human beings are plagued with curiosity. We go afield as idea-tasters to many a table. A sizeable number are clustering around eastern gurus. "Reincarnation" is the Now Thing. Persons who haven't as yet heard a fervent exposition of the subject need only wait a week or two for the topic to come blowing in the wind with all the signs of the Zodiac affixed.

Recently, my friends and I heard Carl, the most voluble member of our Sunday school class, expound. "The more I read about reincarnation," he said, "the more plausible it sounds. Where's there room for all the spirits anyway if they don't recycle into new bodies? Of course they could go off into space, but then — well, I don't cotton to that idea. I like to keep my own close by."

When laughter rippled through the room, Carl looked over the rim of his glasses and, pointing his finger at each of us in turn, admonished us, "Don't be so high and mighty. Just look at Luke 9:18 and 19."

When no one made a move to do so, all of us waiting for Carl to continue, he said, "I mean it! Open your Bibles now."

We did, and followed with our eyes what Carl read aloud slowly and emphatically:

Now it happened that as he was praying alone the disciples were with him; and he asked them, "Who do the people say that I am?" And they answered, *"John the Baptist; but others say Elijah; and others, that one of the old prophets has risen."*

(Luke 9:18, 19)

Carl closed his Bible, adjusted his glasses, and said, "Those folks must have believed in reincarnation, so —"

Julia broke the silence that followed. (She's our ardent recruiter for the Adult Education class in Landscape Painting.) "Sure would be good," she said, "if some of us could have another chance on earth. We'd know then to start painting earlier in life and not wait until we're as old as Grandma Moses was — that is if we could remember then in that second chance all we know now."

The "thin veil." We were talking about that. How far have we roamed? Around the world and in and out of certain minds. We come back to it now, for it is the thin but impenetrable veil, much stronger than the Bamboo Curtain, far more impregnable than the one of iron, that daily and in sleepless hours of the night we widows strain to break through.

In the early months of widowhood most of our thoughts and all of our yearnings are like homing pigeons, our objective fixed on that "veil." Some widows sample the occult, read books on ESP, go to lectures on psychiatric research, or even enroll in courses in para-psychology now being offered by colleges and universities.

During my first months of widowhood,

I did my searching in books. At our local library the cards in every volume dealing with mysticism and life after death bore my name. Always I searched for a personal breakthrough. The longing worked itself into my prayers. At first timidly, gently, "Just some little glimpse, Lord." When that was not granted, my prayers became battering rams. But the "space between" remained unassailable, and the bitterness of frustration threatened the peace I had been claiming from "In my Father's house. . . ." Until —

Until that day when in a quiet moment, still as the eye of a hurricane, words heard weeks before surfaced. Three months before Elam died, Victor, our older son, physicist then at the Atomic Energy installation at Oak Ridge, Tennessee, and his family were with us for a short vacation in Redlands, California. One evening Victor said to Elam and me, "If ever I'm allowed to tell you what's going on at Oak Ridge you'll be amazed, dumbfounded."

"If ever I'm allowed" — these were the words that came back to me after Elam's death, words that started a chain reaction of thoughts. "If . . . allowed." That meant that men, for their own purposes in Oak Ridge, were closing doors of communication. And if men did that, then why shouldn't God, for His own purposes, also do that?

But there was more: some message for me, unspoken, hidden. "If ever. . . ." A fresh thought flashed: But even when Victor might be free to tell, I would not be able to understand. His experiences at Oak Ridge were far beyond my understanding, his vocabulary beyond my comprehension.

My thoughts raced toward the analogy: Even if the closure between Here and There were taken away and Elam could communicate freely with me, how could I understand? Life there being in another dimension, surely the vocabulary must be far removed from the languages of earth.[2]

Yet, in spite of rationalizations, our cries continue: "Why? Why can't they speak to us?" It is the same cry as that of the poet who was inspired by the mystical quality of the paintings of El Greco, the Spanish painter (1541-1614), "in which the human body is elongated and distorted into flame-like shapes suggesting the enormous upward tug of the spirit."[3]

EL GRECO

See how the sun has somewhat not
*   of light*
Falling upon those men who stand so tall;
See how their eyes observe some in-
*   ward sight*
And see how their living takes no room
*   at all,*
Their passing stirs no air, so thin
*   they are;*

*Behind them see small houses with
     small doors;*
The light comes from an unfamiliar star
*That lights their walls and falls across
     their floors.*

*What shall we say when one of those
     men goes*
Into his house and we no longer see
*His eyes observing something that
     he knows,*
And if those houses brim with radiancy
*Why does no light come through as
     those doors close?*[4]

Of these last lines John Ciardi writes:
"The poet . . . is driven to ask a question
of those other-worldly men. If they so
yearn to enter the house of eternity
(whose doorway is the tomb), and if that
house of eternity is full of such radiance
as they envision, then — and each syl-
lable of the line pounds the question —
*why does no light come through as those
doors close?*"[5]

This question is our question too.
Why? Why? Why?

And yet is this a fair question? Does
no light come through? Are we looking
for the kind of light we have here on
earth? Or better put, the kind of light
our eyes see? Are we listening for the
words we know here on earth? Or better
put, the words audible to our present
body's ears? Surely the Creator of heaven
and earth and all the stars and far-flung
universes has more than one model, one
blueprint.

When my own longing for a spoken
word comes on strong — and the longing
still comes, in spite of that flash of truth
from Victor — I parry it with a battery of
questions:

When Elam was here on earth, did I
always need a word to assure me of his
nearness?

Did he not often tell me more in a look,
in a gentle touch than a word could
have told?

When he came home from a trip, didn't
he often tell me he'd felt me near though
separated by a thousand miles? And
didn't I tell him that I had felt the same?

Ah, but it's different now, quite different. He no longer comes home. For more
than a quarter century he has not returned from a long trip, though at times
I've felt his presence so close the tempta-
tion comes: If I turn now I'll surely see
him. But there has been no return —
never a sight, never a sound.

Yet, there have been times of cogni-
tion. Often the perception has come after
the fact. Then I recall that lovely story
of the disciples' walk to Emmaus after
Jesus' crucifixion:

---

*While they were talking and discussing
together, Jesus himself drew near and
went with them. But their eyes were
kept from recognizing him. . . . [Later]
When he was at table with them, he
took the bread and blessed, and broke
it, and gave it to them. And their eyes*

were opened and they recognized him; and he vanished out of their sight. They said to each other, "Did not our hearts burn within us while he talked to us on the road, while he opened to us the scriptures?"

(Luke 24: 15, 16, 30-32)

At times the communing comes in the least likely of places, the most improbable of times, and in the strangest of ways. In the early years I was tempted to dismiss the circumstances of a "meeting" as sheer coincidences. And perhaps some have been and I've made them "meetings" only through wishful thinking. But some must definitely have come to pass through logistics beyond human design.

Take, for instance, that rainy November day when I sat at a lunch counter in a dreary bus restaurant miles away from home. Outside, the sky was overcast with dark clouds. Inside, the room was clouded with cigarette smoke and saturated with the odors of fried onion, hamburger, and burnt toast. Within myself, self-pity and loneliness shrouded my spirit.

"No menu," I said to the waiter. "Just a cup of coffee," wondering whether I'd be able to drink even half.

A hand reached across the person sitting next to me and dropped a coin into the music selector. "Oh no, not that too," I groaned inwardly.

But the first notes were not the rock and roll I had anticipated. Out of that music box came a baritone voice singing an old familiar song, the words filling the room: "I love you truly, truly, dear." The song that Elam had hummed to me the night he told me he loved me!

However did that song get into a cassette of rock and roll? How did it happen to be on target at that particular moment? By coincidence? I think not. Which negation may seem to imply that I credit Elam for this conjunction. I'm not saying that. I'm merely saying that communication may come in strange and diverse ways. Sometimes it would appear then that God himself acts as the middleman.

In recent writings there are choice passages bearing testimony to other widows' experiences of communication. Fresh from yesterday's reading is the story of what happened to Taylor Caldwell three days after the death of her husband Marcus Reback, to whom she had been married for forty years. He had not professed belief in an afterlife, but before he died he promised that if there was such a life, he would return and give a sign. Shortly after the funeral service, the housekeeper called Miss Caldwell to come to the backyard. "There in the yard, blooming for the first time since it had been planted twenty-one years before, was a shrub of Resurrection Lilies" in a blaze of white, "every bud on the plant had burst into glorious fragrance."[6]

Daphne du Maurier's was not an experience of sight, but of feeling:

As the months pass and the seasons change, something of tranquility descends, and although the well-remembered footstep will not sound again, nor the voice call from the room beyond, there seems to be about me in the air an atmosphere of love, a living presence.

It is as though one shared, in some indefinable manner, the freedom and the peace, even at times the joy, of another world, where there is no pain.

When Christ, the healer, said, "Blessed are they that mourn, for they shall be comforted," he must have meant just this.[7]

Clarissa Start tells of her experience on a shopping tour, of all places — on an escalator. "Suddenly a feeling peaceful and loving came, as if someone were with me."[8]

Pearl Buck, in her book *A Bridge for Passing*, writes:

I opened the window and sent my secret message into space with love. Wherever he is, he heard, or so I dreamed, for a new comfort descended upon my heart and brought to me my first intimation of eventual peace. It was his blessing.[9]

C. S. Lewis in *A Grief Observed* describes his own experience of "meeting" his wife after her death:

It's the quality of last night's experience — not what it proves but what it was — that makes it worth putting down. It was quite incredibly unemotional. Just the impression of her mind momentarily facing my own. Mind, not "soul" as we tend to think of soul. Certainly the reverse of what is called "soulful". Not at all like a rapturous re-union of lovers. Much more like getting a telephone call or a wire from her about some practical arrangement. Not that there was any "message" — just intelligence and attention. No sense of joy or sorrow. No love even, in our ordinary sense. No unlove. I had never in any mood imagined the dead as being so — well, so business-like. Yet there was an extreme and cheerful intimacy. An intimacy that had not passed through the senses or the emotions at all.[10]

To these witnessings comes one more, that of Elizabeth Gray Vining:

The tragedy of death, as someone wiser than I has said, is separation, but even separation may not be permanent. The sense of continuing companionship with those who have gone beyond the horizon which comes to me occasionally makes me confident that someday we shall see beyond the mystery which now we must accept.[11]

For periods of days I go with no sensation whatsoever of Elam's presence. After such a period I wrote:

Silence

This awful silence after death! It spreads
Around me like a wintry steppe. She
Is brave indeed who never fears or
    dreads
That lonely place where mortal eye
    can see
No sign of life; where nothing is that
    breathes
Save self; where even long-familiar stars
Recede and, in the coldness, funeral
    wreaths
Again are heaped against the bolted bars.
Yes, brave indeed who neither dreads
    nor fears
The silence after death. I am not brave.
The times of hollow emptiness
    bring tears,
And life ends there beside your distant
    grave.

But, God, let not my heart to doubt
    be bound.
Let Silence be my faith's last proving
    ground!

Then come days when his presence fills the house. I feel him everywhere. Without benefit of speech I absorb his thoughts. A time like that inspired:

Speech

At times you speak to me, not word
    by word
As once you spoke, but thought by
    thought. I feel
Ideas flashing by like chimney bird
That on a sickle wing takes evening
    meal —
The same sure, sudden flight through
    air,
The silent streak of swiftly moving life
That's scarcely felt before it is no
    longer there.

As keen and instant as a surgeon's knife,
So come your thoughts at times to me —
    complete,
When, flashing through the silence of
    the night,
Whole volumes that you never once
    repeat
Impinge upon my mind with speed of
    light.

Your speech is now a new and different
    thing
And yet as real as is the swallow's wing.

The veil between the living and the dead — how inexorably it separates!
And yet at times, how very thin it seems.

The Quickening

The Quickening

This morning Vicki phoned, "Will you be home tonight?"

"Yes. Can you come for supper? Just the two of us. We'll have waffles.".

"I'd love to, and I'm glad we'll be alone. I have something to show you, something about — but wait. I'll bring it when I come. It's something I'm excited about."

Excited! It was the first time since Bill's death, six months ago, I'd heard her use that word. Before he died she was always excited about something or other: bubbling over about their plan to remodel the kitchen; rushing off to a class in calligraphy — "Going to make our own cards this Christmas," or replanting the borders — "Annuals out, perennials in." Always busy about something exciting. *Joie de vivre* ran full and free through her being.

For the past month there had been no such joy, no sparkle of excitement in her blue eyes.

Now, though, the lilt in her voice over the phone gave evidence of a greening at the margins of her grief and held promise of a return to the challenge of living.

That lilt brought to my mind the feeling I had had seven months after Elam's death, when I experienced my first sustained upsurge of spirit. The exact date is forgotten, but memory has repeatedly pulled me to the place — a certain spot between the bus depot and the bungalow in Redlands that was now my home — and to the time — one twilight hour in spring.

I had spent the day in Claremont, California, matriculating for a doctorate in Far East Studies at the graduate school there. My goal: to teach at college. Through the friendly guidance of Dr. S. Y. Chen, there was now in my arms a package containing a Chinese language book, a box of Chinese character cards, and two history books. A heavy package, but as I started on that walk homeward from the depot, the package became light in weight. *Almost as though Elam were helping me carry it,* I thought.

Maybe he was! For now I was on the road, not only of fulfilling my own latent dream of teaching again — "again" because home and children and responsibilities connected with Elam's position had interrupted my teaching — but also of fulfilling Elam's too. "Someday," he once had confided, "when I finish with administrative work, I'd like to get back into classroom teaching."

With that double hope came a sudden burst of excitement, a catch of joy within me, a definite quickening comparable to the three quickenings I had experienced years ago. Those three marked life for our three children. This quickening was marking the renewal of life for me.

It was something akin to this that I had been watching for in Vicki, praying for because I knew that only when the bereaved comes upon some idea, some activity, some project, some challenge, or some person who needs her, will she move outside herself. Only then will she be on the road to wholeness. By her words, "I'm excited," it would appear that one or more of these discoveries had now come to Vicki. For that I thanked God.

Now she was watching me as I put the first ladle of batter onto the waffle griddle. "Any idea what I brought to show you?" she asked. No mistaking the sparkle in her eyes.

I glanced at her trim figure in the dark blue jumper over a plaid skirt. "Your new dress with the mod layered look. It's beautiful."

"New?" She smiled and shrugged her shoulders. "Only if you call wearing two made-over dresses 'new.' No, it's this." She reached into her handbag, then hesitated, closed the bag and said, "Later. After the waffles." Inhaling the fragrance of the first one fresh from the griddle, she added, "Waffles deserve full attention now."

Before our second cup of coffee she reached into her bag again. "Can't wait any longer for you to see this," she said, handing me a clipping from the *Houston Post*. "It came in the mail this morning. Something Bill's sister found while researching for her thesis. Almost a year since it was printed, but the news is fresh to me. Why haven't we heard about it before this? Read it. Read it out loud."

I set down my cup and read:

WIDOW TO WIDOW

It Helps to Talk About Loneliness and All the Other Problems Death Brings

"If only I had someone to talk with, someone who understands," pleads a widow.

"It's so lonely," adds another.

"Doctors load you with tranquilizers and tell you you'll be all right. [Like my doctor, I thought, hearing again his

words, "You're strong. You'll make it."]
That doesn't help."

"The house is so empty. I'm lonely."
. . . "You're a fifth wheel. Your friends
are nice but. . . . You're just alone."[1]

I looked up. Vicki was nodding her
head. "Just what I've been saying, isn't
it? Go on."

These are widows talking, eagerly
sharing experiences and problems, reaching out to help others and to be helped
in a time of need.

These persons are doing something
about that loneliness and the other problems widowed women and men face.
They answered a call to be volunteers
with Widowed, Inc., a new service organization which aims to help persons
adjust when they lose a mate.

Shirley Wolfer, executive director, started Widowed, Inc. in Houston. She lost
her husband 16 months ago and while
staying with relatives in Boston discovered how helpful the Widow to Widow
program[2] there was.

She returned to Houston, her home,
and began calling on friends and associ-
ates with service agencies, lawyers,
businessmen, psychiatrists, job counse-
lors, and others who could give sound
advice to the widowed.

A board of directors was formed and a
call for volunteers brought out more
than 50 persons at the organizational
meeting.[3]

"See why I'm excited?" Vicki interrupted. "If someone in Houston can set
up a group like that, what's to stop us
from setting up one here?"

"What indeed?" I paused, lost in the
memory of that hour, years ago, when I
needed someone to talk to — not just
anyone, but someone who had gone
through the same experience I had gone
through. It was during my first term at
Claremont. From Mondays to Fridays I
had a room and kitchen privileges in a
private home. Weekends I was at home
in Redlands with my mother and younger
son. One weekday evening when I was
eating my solitary meal on the porch in
Claremont, I was caught in a flood of
loneliness. Across town lived the widow
of a college president who had died
shortly before Elam. Elam had known
him as a colleague, but I had met her
only once at a reception. She wouldn't
remember me, yet I longed to go to her.
Above all other persons she would know
my particular loneliness. Just to talk
with her would be a comfort. For an
hour I debated: To go or not to go. In the
end I stayed where I was, thinking, If
only we had a banding together of widows, a Widows Anonymous to help
each other.

Now here was a clipping that report-
ed just such an organization. I'd been a
quarter of a century too early.

"Read on," Vicki urged. "Where have
you been the past minute?"

"In Claremont," I answered.

Glancing ahead, I saw that one aim of Widowed, Inc. is to guide persons to proper counseling in financial and legal matters. "That," I said, finding my own excitement equaling Vicki's, "is a real service."

"Exactly right! And look at that." I looked. Her finger pointed to the next lines:

"I lost some of my credit cards because I was honest and told the companies my husband had died. They sent me applications for a new card and when they saw I had no job, they didn't give me one," Mrs. Wolfer says.

"You're thrown out of society. You can't go out like you used to. You're a prisoner in your home."[4]

Turning to me, her eyes looking directly into mine, excitement replaced by wistfulness, Vicki asked, "Tell me, how long does it take before you feel free?"

"What do you mean 'free'?"

"Feel free about going out. Not feel like a fifth wheel when you're in a crowd of couples. Not self-conscious when you go into a restaurant alone."

"Well," I stalled, "that depends upon the person. The Chinese have a good saying, *I-ko jen yu i-ko jen-di p'i-ch'i* (Each person has his own disposition). So, some feel free sooner than others, some later, some never."

The rest of the news item dealt with children. Seeing me hesitate, Vicki said, "No need to pass up that part. Early in marriage when we found we could not have children, Bill and I thought of adopting two, but adoptions are not so easy these days. Always something that interfered. I love children, and I've found that I can do a lot for some of them without adopting them. Right now I'm glad I don't have the responsibility for rearing a child alone."

The article quoted one widowed mother as saying, "Children can be life savers and heart breakers when a mate is lost." One said, "I don't know what I would have done without mine." Another said, "Children also put you over the barrel."

The article concluded:

What Widowed, Inc. hopes to say by its actions is, "You're not alone in your feelings. Thousands of others are just like you."[5]

"So now —" Vicki reached for the clipping, "you see why I'm excited and why I brought this to you. Can't you and I do for our town what is being done in Houston and in Boston? I'm ready to start. Are you?"

"Ready? I should have set up this kind of a helping organization myself a quarter of a century ago. When do we begin?"

Renewal

Renewal

After Vicki left, I sat by my open fire thinking of her new enthusiasm and feeling my own excitement for our mutual endeavor. As I watched the last of the fir logs turn to embers, suddenly there came a crackling sound and a bright flame. Within the small unburned section of log hidden among the ashes there must have been a pocket of resin locked fast until almost all of the wood was consumed.

Like the flame, there leapt to my mind a verse from Psalms:

My heart was hot within me, and while I was thus musing the fire kindled.
(Psalm 39:4)[1]

How like a fire kindling among smoldering ash was Vicki's enthusiasm for this new project, Widows, Inc. or Widow-to-Widow Program, whatever the name would be! It would draw her out of herself. It would involve her with persons, bringing to them warmth and comfort, strength and encouragement, and to herself that particular heart's joy that comes from an unselfish and loving concern for others.

At the center of the project was the word "behold," the word that Jesus had said to mourners close to the cross:

When Jesus saw his mother, and the disciple whom he loved standing near, he said to his mother, "Woman, behold your son!" Then he said to the disciple, "Behold, your mother!" And from that hour the disciple took her to his own home.
(John 19:26, 27)

In that unembellished word "behold" the picture of Mary and John at the foot of the cross comes clear and near in three dimensions — two persons assigned to comfort each other.

Biblical scholars indicate that the "behold" used in the verses above is the Greek word *idou* translated as "See! Lo!"

Lo brings the aura of sympathy, compassion, concern, caring. It is the *lo* in

"*. . . and lo, I am with you always, to the close of the age.*"

(Matthew 28:20)

Behold one another. Comfort one another. Care for one another. These are admonitions given in both the Old and the New Testaments:

Comfort, comfort my people, says your God.

(Isaiah 40:1)

Bear one another's burdens, and so fulfil the law of Christ.

(Galatians 6:2)

To Jews and Christians alike, concern for others is a fundamental tenet of faith.

It is for people of other faiths too. The tender story told in *Light of Asia* of the Hindu mother bringing her child to Buddha to be healed bears repeating. Unaware that the child in her arms is already dead, the sorrowing mother comes to Buddha to beg a tola of black mustard seed from any household untouched by death. This seed is for the healing of her child. When she fails to find one single house where death has not come, as Buddha knew she would, he says to her:

"*My sister! thou hast found . . .*
Searching for what none finds — that

bitter balm
I had to give thee . . . . today
Thou know'st the whole wide world
 weeps with thy woe;
The grief which all hearts share grows
 less for one."[2]

Now Vicki was hearing *idou* for herself: Behold other widows! From her experience she had found, as through the years I had found, that only a widow knows best what another widow is facing. We need no further proof of this truth than that given in a comment the week before by one of Vicki's married neighbors. This woman's husband had work that took him away from home for weeks at a time.

"Sometimes for two and three months," the neighbor lamented. "I'm afraid all the time he's gone. I keep thinking, What if something happens? What if —"

"Yes, I know it must be hard," Vicki sympathized. "But your husband comes back to you. He's alive. You're not like me."

"Oh, but it's easier for you," came the neighbor's quick reply. "Your husband's gone once and for all. You don't have to worry anymore."

Such blindness of spirit! Not limited, either, to wives like the above. Dr. Phyllis Silverman writes, "Widows I have talked with felt that neither friends, family, physicians, nor clergymen, for that matter, were very helpful. All wanted them to recover as quickly as possible,"[3] far earlier than the trauma of grief would allow. They seem incapable of giving sympathy in depth; their feelings of compassion wear thin too soon.

"True understanding," widows say, "comes only from other widows. They are the ones who come to sit beside you, holding your hand, sometimes not saying more than 'I know, I know.' And at the time that's all that's needed."

The power of the comfort of these words struck me again the other day when my five-year-old neighbor girl, Kelli, stood weeping at my door. "My bird is dead. My bird is dead." Her words were muffled in sobs. "It'll never sing for me again. It's dead."

I drew her into the house, led her to the davenport, and sat beside her, holding her close. Her small body was wracked with grief.

"I know. I know." Softly spoken, my words were measured to her sobs, like responses in a Litany for the Sorrowing.

After a while, Kelli's sobs subsided. Came a few shuddering breaths, and then, rubbing the tears from her cheeks with the palms of her small hands, she drew from my embrace, stood up, announced, "I feel better now," and went home.

This "I feel better now" is what we had as the goal for gathering together a few widows to present a plan patterned after Widow-to-Widow Program or Widows, Inc. I would invite Dora and Mamie and Julia, all in their first year of widowhood. Vicki would invite Joan.

Dora, in her late thirties, has two girls and a boy, ranging in age from eight to twelve. She teaches in grade school — began teaching when her youngest entered first grade and has been teaching ever since. Her husband died eight months ago while on a business trip to Mexico. His body was found in the hotel room. When the diagnosis came, "Heart," she could not believe it. "Just before he left," she said, staring into space, "our doctor said he was in perfect health. How could it be?"

Mamie is in her seventies. She has five children, all married, ten grandchildren, and five great-grandchildren. Each child would like Mamie to make her home with him or her, but Mamie prefers living alone in the house where she and her husband Fred had lived since they were married more than fifty years ago and where he died five months ago. Although she is older than any of the others, she is youngest in her widowhood.

Fred had been a semi-invalid for a long time. Most of the past few months of his life were spent on the couch in the living room. His only exercise was walking among his plants on the long back porch, which years ago he had made into a home conservatory.

Looking at the couch, the pillow plumped,

the afghan carefully folded, Mamie says, "It still seems he's just out there with his plants taking a little walk, talking to them and giving them a little loving — but now he never comes back."

Mamie is not the only widow who for short minutes at a time harbors the feeling "He's just away." Others have said the same. Shortly after President Roosevelt's death, Eleanor Roosevelt wrote to President Truman, "It is still difficult to believe my husband is not off on a trip."[4] Once after Elam's death, before I moved from the home on the campus, I heard a car coming up the road behind the house, the road Elam always used to take. Joy filled my heart, as it always had at that sound. I leaned to look out the window and thought, *Oh, it's Elam coming home!* Then the car passed by the window, a stranger at the wheel.

Julia, the third of the guests I would invite, and Bert, her husband, had had a once-in-a-lifetime day last May. Not only were they celebrating their own twenty-fifth wedding anniversary, but their daughter and son-in-law were celebrating their fifth, and their son was bringing them, through marriage, another daughter. When Bert died in June, the potted plants from that happy May day were still blooming in Julia's garden.

Last week Vicki had heard of a Vietnam widow who had moved into her neighborhood. "Could you call on her with me?" Of course I could.

We found Joan Roberts, young and very beautiful, far more self-possessed than we thought she would be. She told us her husband had been killed in Vietnam three years ago when she was twenty-two. Those two facts made her the youngest in years among us, but, except for myself, the oldest in widowhood.

"But when you hear that I'm going to be married to my husband's best friend when he returns from Vietnam, you may not want me," she said.

"Oh, yes, we do," Vicki assured her. "You'll be willing to share won't you? Or would it be too — too painful?"

"No. If you think my experience can help anyone, I'll be glad to come."

So now we had four. With Vicki and myself we'd be six. She set the date for Tuesday evening, two weeks before Christmas. "And I want us to meet at my house," she said. That would be the first time since Bill's death that she'd be having a group. It was another healthful sign.

On Monday the day before that Tuesday our local paper carried an announcement of a new shop, "Marietta's," being opened in a country home close to town. The advertisement read, "Christmas gifts from around the world."

Christmas and all things pertaining to it trigger an extra flow of adrenalin in me, so Tuesday morning there I was at the shop, eye-and-finger-deep in tinsel and sparkle, dolls and toys, games and books gathered from Tokyo to Timbuktu.

Marietta, whose age I could not guess — she being in features, complexion, and bearing one of those women who remain ageless — had inherited the farm from a great-aunt. Now, initially stocking it with trinkets and *objets d'art* gathered on several world cruises with her husband, she had turned three rooms of the house into a gift shop. More gifts were being ordered. "My husband's hobby was travel," she said. "Mine was compulsive buying."

"Your husband — is he in business with you?" I asked.

"No." She paused. "No, he's dead."

Impulsively I invited her to meet with us at Vicki's that night.

"Delighted to come. Please make a map for me."

At Vicki's front door that evening I had to practice control over *my* tears. She had a lighted wreath in the window and on the door a swag of fir and holly with bells made from small tin cans. I was staring at the bells when she opened the door. "Not as large as Christina's fruit juice cans," she said, "but these smaller cans made better bells."

"Oh, Vicki, you darling!" My arms went around her.

Inside, looking at our gathered guests, I saw how diverse were our ages. From twenty-five-year-old Joan through ageless Marietta to Mamie and myself, we represented a range of over fifty years. But a widow is a widow, no matter what her age.

As a starter Vicki told the group about Widows, Inc., and I brought information about the Widow-to-Widow Program in Boston which I had learned about that afternoon in the library. Both programs are self-help programs. The helpers are widows who themselves have "lived through the crisis . . . recovered, and . . . teach others that it can be done and how to do it."[5] These widows are called "caregivers." Their training comes not from formal courses, but from their own experiences. Their claim, "I know what it is like. Let me help you," brings comfort and fresh courage to the mourner. One widow spoke for many when she said to a caregiver:

"Since you are a widow, too, when you said you understand I knew you meant it and that was so important. I can't stand sympathy and that's all anyone else could give me."[6]

Then Vicki told of her hope to begin a program here in our town. "And maybe some of you will volunteer to be caregivers," she said. "Think about it. We'll have another meeting after Christmas. Then you can give your answer.

"For tonight let's just get acquainted and share with each other what we have done or are doing or plan to do to become a whole person again." Turning to me she asked, "How did you express it the other night?"

"Coming to the growing edge," I said, "or call it renewal."

As the sharing progressed, one axiom became clear: Either you work towards approaching a new growing edge, toward becoming a whole person again, or you spend some time in a sanitarium, if you can afford it, or else you just make life miserable for yourself and for everyone around you. Anyone who dawdles in self-pity is useless to herself and alienates herself from others.

Dora was grateful for having children and her teaching. "I don't know what I'd do without either of them. Not that they wholly take away the ache and the loneliness, but having responsibilities automatically programs my hours."

When she stopped, I took from my purse a copy of the poem she had written a month after her husband's death. I had brought it along hoping she might be willing to share it. Now I held it toward her saying, "Would you read this for us?"

"You read it," she said.

So I read Dora's

Blueprint for Widowhood

Push them to the back of your mind.
Don't be caught unaware, don't let your
*   thoughts go too deep —*
Think only of the chores to be finished,
*   the trivia of the daily routine.*
Smile brightly, laugh, even when the
*   laughter is only*
A surface reflection of an inner tension.
Talk, talk, talk — don't take time for
*   solitude —*
You might find yourself listening for a
*   remembered footstep.*
Hurry! Turn on the radio; let the pound-
*   ing of the drum*
And the bass fiddle mask the thudding
*   of your heart beat.*
Look to today or tomorrow.
Don't let the memories of yesterday
*   flood in.*
Their bittersweetness can
*   overwhelm you.*
Be careful — don't let down your
*   defenses.*

Keep busy with projects and meetings.
Go to bed so tired that the yearning for
*   a familiar touch*
Can be suppressed by fatigue and then
*   by the escape of sleep.*

Avoid the pain of remembering, the
*   hurt of loneliness.*
Run, girl, run . . .

All around the circle, heads were nodding empathy with that feeling.

Soon after she had arrived, Mamie started knitting on a red sweater. Now she laid down her knitting and said, "I too had that feeling and often still have it, but my knees don't let me run very far, so I run with my hands. Knitting caps and scarfs and sweaters for our mission in Alaska brings me comfort."

Turning to me, she added, "I often think of what your mother said to me that day our mission circle met in your home. She was close to ninety-five then, wasn't she?"

I nodded.

"She gave us her translation of something Dr. Schweitzer once said: 'Busy hands motor the troubled mind.' I've found that to be true. And just the other day my daughter read me something Mrs. Roosevelt wrote after her husband died. I've brought the book with me. This is the part."

I met, as so many women have met, the loneliness that can be so devastating, if one permits it to be, . . . But I discovered that by keeping as busy as possible I could manage increasingly to keep my loneliness at bay. The advantage of being busy is that you don't have time to think about yourself.[7]

Vicki, next to Mamie, had been looking at Mamie's sweater. "Such beautiful, even knitting," she said now.

"Mamie, your middle name ought to be Dorcas after the widow in the Bible who was so 'full of good works and acts of charity.'"[8]

"And for being led 'through the valley of the shadow of death,'"[9] Mamie added, "as Dorcas was raised from the valley itself.[10] Deep sorrow comes close to death."

Then Mamie reached for her knitting and again fingers and needles moved in rhythm.

Julia broke the short silence that followed. When Bert was living, she seldom drove their car, but she often went with him on trips he made for FISH, taking elderly and handicapped persons to appointments or shopping. Now she was driving alone. "Kind of taking his place," she said. "I get comfort out of doing it for him."

At first Joan was a bit shy. She repeated for the group what she had told Vicki and me about her plans for marriage. "So, you see, I shouldn't be here."

"Oh, yes, you should," Dora spoke up. "Getting married again won't erase your memory of how you've felt as a widow. Those first weeks after —" Dora put her hand to her mouth. One could see she hadn't meant to go that far.

"Those first weeks after the news," Joan picked up the sentence, "were the hardest I've ever gone through. Jim and I had known each other since we were young children. There never was any one else for either of us. When he was drafted, we decided to get married. Six months later he was in Vietnam. A month from then he was killed in action."

She looked around as though to test us. Could she fully open her heart to us? Satisfied, she confided, "Strange, frightening thoughts came. I was horrified myself at wishing I were a Hindu widow in the years when suttee was practiced in India. I'd gladly have died on a pyre with Jim, but there was no pyre either here or in Vietnam. A land mine is not a blazing fire." She stopped, shuddered slightly, and then went on. "I thought of suicide. I was convinced in my own mind that I couldn't live without Jim. I had it all worked out, just how and when and where. But, thank God, 'Operation Second Life' saved me.

"That's what a Navy psychiatrist launched for us Vietnam widows to help us over 'the first shock and later depression, self-incrimination, self-pity, and the feeling of helplessness.'[11]

"If only the thousands of Vietnam war widows could have what my small group of thirty had! We learned there how to change from being a widow to being a single woman again. Not easy, but necessary if we were to go on living any kind of productive life. And now," she looked around the circle, a smile on her lips and in her eyes, "now will you all come to my wedding?"

After a brief noisy session about Joan's plans and our promise for 100 percent attendance at the wedding, Vicki called on Marietta.

"You've all been so frank," Marietta said. "You make it easy for me to speak from my heart. The past year was the hardest year of my life. My husband was much older than I am. He was wealthy. He treated me like a queen — no, better than a queen. I had no responsibilities. No budget to balance. No work to do. We traveled a lot. Life was one good time after another.

"Suddenly everything changed. I'll never understand how it happened, but one day the ugly word bankruptcy rocked my world. Everything we had went into that word. The next week my husband" — she paused as though to choose the word. She settled for "died," though her pause gave the impression that the full truth lay in another word.

"Then my world was completely shattered. The bottom fell out. There was no insurance for me — unbelievable, but true. All I had to start a new life with were the mementos of our travels. Why they were not claimed by law I could not at first understand. But when my great-aunt's legacy came, I saw God's hand in the sparing. Those mementos, I hope, will prove to be for me what the jar of oil was for the widow who cried to Elisha

---

"Your servant my husband is dead; and you know that your servant feared the Lord, but the creditor has come to take my two children to be his slaves."

(2 Kings 4:1)

I'm hoping the merchandise I now have will be the starter, the primer, for a business that will pay all my debts and bring in enough for me to live on."

Marietta's frankness touched all of us. The silence that followed was a tribute to her trust in us and to her courage.

Julia broke the silence, laying her hand on Marietta's and saying, "First thing tomorrow I'm coming out to your shop." Then turning to Vicki, she said, "You haven't told us what your project is."

"Forming groups like this." Vicki spread out her hands as though to touch each of us. "I want to do for our town and our state what's being done in Massachusetts and Texas and a few other places. I'm hoping you'll all volunteer to become caregivers.

"But that's not all. I'm also going to enroll at the university next term for training in work with handicapped children."

Then looking straight at me, she challenged, "And you, what more are you planning to do to keep on that growing edge you like to talk about? Write another book? You've done one for retirees. How about one for widows?"

Another book! That would take effort and time. How much of each does an eighty-one-year-old still have? In the moment of hesitation before answering, there came the familiar warning of new life — another quickening.

"Well, now," I said, "I just might do that. I know a good beginning:

How lonely sits the city
  that was full of people!
How like a widow has she become.
(Lamentations 1:1)

---

and I know a good ending:

Remember my affliction and my
  bitterness, the wormwood and
  the gall! . . .

But this I call to mind,
  And therefore I have hope:

The steadfast love of the Lord never
  ceases, his mercies never come
  to an end;
they are new every morning;
  great is thy faithfulness.
(Lamentations 3:19, 21-23)

This I can say from my heart, for I know it is true.

"With a beginning and an ending, all I'll have to do is write the in-between. Yes, Vicki, I just might do that. With all of you to help me, it can't be too difficult."

This is the book.

Notes

Chapter 2

1. William Merrill, *The Interpreter's Bible* (Abingdon Press, 1956), Vol. VI, p. 6. Used by permission of the publisher.

2. Pearl Buck, *A Bridge for Passing* (The John Day Co., 1962), p. 96.

3. Charlotte Montgomery, "Speaker for the House," *Good Housekeeping* (September, 1972), pp. 30, 31.

4. John Morton Blum, *Diaries of Henry Morgenthau, Jr. 1928-1938* (Houghton Mifflin Co., 1959), p. 424. Used by permission of publisher.

5. Fr. H. Himmel, *Deutsche Heimat* herausgegeben Von L. Andersen (Mainz und Leipzig: B. Schott's Söhne), p. 30.

6. C.S. Lewis, *A Grief Observed* (Copyright ©, 1961, by N.W. Clerk), pp. 11-13. Used by permission of the publisher, Seabury Press.

7. Alvin Toffler, *Future Shock* (Bantam Book Paperback, 1970), p. 329. Used by permission of Random House, Inc.

8. Daphne du Maurier, "Life Without Him," *Good Housekeeping* (November, 1966), p. 93.

9. Clarissa Start, *When You're a Widow* (Copyright by Clarissa Start, 1968), pp. 42, 43. Used by permission of Concordia Publishing House.

Chapter 3

1. Faith Baldwin, "Couples," from *Widow's Walk* (Copyright by Faith Baldwin Cutrell, 1954), p. 17. Used by permission of Holt, Rinehart and Winston, Inc.

2. Start, *op. cit.*, p. 87.

3. I.B. Sergei, "My God and I" (© 1935, renewed © 1963 by Austris A. Wihtol). Used by permission of Singspiration Music, a Division of The Zondervan Corporation.

4. Statistical Abstract of the United States:

Marital Status of Population: By Sex and Age, 1970

	Actual Female (millions aged 14 & over)	Percent
Total	77.2	100%
Single	17.1	22.1%
Married	47.8	62 %
Widowed	9.64 (Approximately) (10,000,000)	12.5%
Divorced	2.695	3.5%

By Age (over 30)		% Married	% Widowed	% Divorced
30 - 34 years	5.8	88.3	0.8	4.6
35 - 44 years	11.8	86.9	2.5	5.4
45 - 54 years	12.1	82	8.1	4.9
55 - 64 years	9.7	67.3	21.3	4.5
65 - 74 years	6.7	45.4	43.7	3.0
75 years and over	4.6	20.9	70.5	1.3

Chapter 4

1. Lady Hosie, *Jesus and Woman* (London: Hodder and Stoughton, Ltd., 1946 and 1949), pp. 25, 26. Used by permission of the Estate of the late Lady Hosie and Hodder and Stoughton, Ltd.

Chapter 5

1. *When Death Steps In*, A Ministry Through Letters to Those Who Truly Loved and Now Freshly Mourn (Privately published, 1956).

Chapter 6

1. Elizabeth Yates, *Up the Golden Stair* (Copyright © 1966 by Elizabeth Yates McGreal), p. 30. Published by E.P. Dutton & Co., Inc. and used with their permission.

2. This experience was first told in *When Death Steps In, op. cit.*, The Fifth Letter, pp. 5, 6.

3. John Ciardi, *How Does a Poem Mean* (Houghton Mifflin Co., 1960), p. 925.

4. E.L. Mayo, quoted in *Ibid.*

5. Ciardi, *op. cit.*

6. Excerpt from *The Search for a Soul* by Jess Stearn (Copyright © 1972, 1973 by Jess Stearn and Taylor Caldwell). Used by permission of Doubleday & Co., Inc.

7. du Maurier, *op. cit.*, pp. 176, 178.

8. Start, *op. cit.*, p. 102.

9. Buck, *op. cit.*, p. 169.

10. Lewis, *op. cit.*, pp. 57, 58.

11. Elizabeth Gray Vining, "My World Was Wrecked Once," in Edward R. Murrow, ed., *This I Believe* (Simon and Schuster, 1952), pp. 183, 184. Used by permission of publisher.

Chapter 7

1. Martha Liebrum, "Widowed, Inc.," *Houston Post,* Wednesday, June 28, 1972, p. 3/AA. Copyright 1972 by *Houston Post* and used by their permission.

2. Widow to Widow Program under the direction of Dr. Phyllis Rolfe Silverman, associated with the Laboratory of Community Psychiatry (Gerald Captain, M.D., Director) of the Department of Psychiatry of Harvard Medical School, 58 Fenwood Road, Boston, Mass. 02115.

3. Liebrum, *op. cit.*

4. *Ibid.*

5. *Ibid.*

Chapter 8

1. Translation as given in *The Book of Common Prayers* (Cambridge: The University Press), p. 394. Numbered here as verse 4. SRV numbers it as verse 3.

2. Matthew Arnold, "The Light of Asia," in Lin Yutang, ed., *The Wisdom of China and India* (Random House, Inc., 1942), p. 445. Used by permission of publisher.

3. Phyllis Rolfe Silverman, Ph.D., "The Widow to Widow Program, An experiment in preventive intervention," *Mental Hygiene,* Vol. 53, no. 3 (July, 1969), p. 334. Used by permission.

4. Joseph P. Lash, *Eleanor: The Years Alone* (Norton, 1972), p. 15.

5. Silverman, *op. cit.,* p. 337.

6. Phyllis Rolfe Silverman, Ph.D., "The Widow as a Caregiver in a Program of Preventive Intervention with Other Widows," *Mental Hygiene,* Vol. 54, no. 4 (October, 1970), p. 542. Used by permission.

7. Eleanor Roosevelt, *You Learn by Living* (Harper and Row, Publishers, Inc., 1960), p. 84. Used by permission of publishers.

8. Acts 9:36.

9. Psalm 23:4.

10. Acts 9:40-42.

11. "Operation Second Life," *Time* (July 25, 1969), pp. 54, 55.

Acknowledgments

I wish to express my appreciation to the publishers listed under *Notes* for permission to use material from their publications; to my typist, Edythe Gunderman, for her patience with me; to Dolores Grundhauser for permission to use her poem "Blueprint for Widowhood"; and to my daughter, Dr. Frances A. Gulick, for her gentle counsel and encouragement.

I would also like to state that although many persons in this book are from real life, there are several mentioned by name who, although resembling in part some of my friends, are mainly characters of my imagination.